SUPERPOWERS OF NATURE

QEB

CONTENTS

INTRODUCTION

This book will help you discover the clever and inventive ways that nature has given birth to heroes.

Many creatures have spectacular powers; there's the squirrel that can fly or the genius octopus with its many mini-brains. But how do animals develop their superpowers? Small changes in DNA alter the way that a species looks or behaves. These changes may be passed down from parents to their offspring. If the changes make the species stronger, the individuals that have inherited them will thrive, while those that have not may die out. This process, called "natural selection," results in the "survival of the fittest." The champions in this book include species that have evolved the sharpest senses or the ability to outrun prey or predators. But they aren't necessarily the strongest, nor have they always crushed all the competition. All of them belong to larger ecosystems, where they play their part for their communities. They are both predators and prey; builders, destroyers, and maintainers. All of them contribute to making our planet amazing.

This book was written by another evolutionary champion: *Homo sapiens*. We humans may not be as gifted in terms of physical performance, but using our excellent brains we have invented ways to fly ever higher, move ever faster, and dive ever deeper. Our next and most important challenge is to find ways to save other species.

Denis ODY, Oceanologist, WWF France

SENSORY WONDERS

It's always tempting to compare the abilities of animals with those of humans.

When it comes to our sensory skills, we tend to be a little big-headed, but a look at the world of living things around us ought quickly to put us in our place! Our eyes are completely different from the eyes of invertebrates, and our sense of smell is laughable compared to a snake's. Bats can hear ultrasound, which humans can't, and through a "lateral line" on their skin, some fish can feel vibrations underwater that are completely unknown to us. In short, when we compare our sensory powers with those of the animal kingdom, a little modesty might be in order!

ELECTRIC EEL

SUPERPOWER:
DANGEROUS VOLTAGE

SUPER STATS:
SCIENTIFIC NAME: *Electrophorus electricus*
Size: 8 feet (2.5 meters) long
Weight: 44 pounds (20 kilograms)
Location: South America

SUPER FACT:
This eel can give electric shocks
of up to 600 volts.

Eels are electric fish! They can give out electric shocks, and are also sensitive to changes in the electric field around them.

The shocks given off by electric eels can reach 600 volts and 2 amps. Another fish that can give an electric shock is the Atlantic torpedo, a species of electric ray; its shock can reach 200 volts and 30 amps. Both eels and torpedoes use their electric charges to deter predators if they get too close, and to stun prey.

Electric eels are also sensitive to the weakest changes—down to one tenth of a microvolt—in the electric field that they create around them. This means they can easily detect prey or obstacles in their path. This ability also plays an important role in their sense of direction, and the ways they talk to one another. Although generally not dangerous to humans, on rare occasions accidents do happen.

TARSIERS

- 💪 **SUPERPOWER:**
  NIGHT VISION

- ⚙️ **SUPER STATS:**
  SCIENTIFIC NAME: *Tarsius*
  FAMILY: *Haplorhini* (dry-nosed primates)
  Size: 6 inches (15 centimeters) excluding tail
  Location: Southeast Asia

- 👍 **SUPER FACT:**
  Tarsiers are the smallest primates
  in the world.

A tarsier is so tiny it could fit in the palm of your hand, but its eyes—at 0.6 inch (1.5 centimeters) in diameter—are huge in relation to the rest of it, and are pretty much fixed in one place. In order to see to the sides or behind, this little creature can rotate its head 180 degrees.

Tarsiers can see in the dark. They eat only at night, when they catch insects or gather plants. Entirely tree-dwelling, they can jump between branches on their springy lower limbs. Three types of bones make up these springs: the tibia and fibula (which are joined together); the tarsal bones (so big and important that the species is named after them); and the long, bendy toe bones. Their toes have pads like suction cups on the ends of them.

Tarsiers are hunted by many predators, but their main enemy is humans. They are almost extinct because of deforestation in Southeast Asia (Malaysia, Indonesia, and the Philippines).

PLATYPUS

SUPERPOWER:
ELECTRICITY
DETECTION

SUPER STATS:
SCIENTIFIC NAME:
Ornithorhynchus anatinus
ORDER: Monotremata
Size: 16–20 inches
(40–50 centimeters) inc. tail
Location: Australia

SUPER FACT:
Like a reptile or a bird,
the female lays eggs,
but she feeds her young
milk like a mammal.

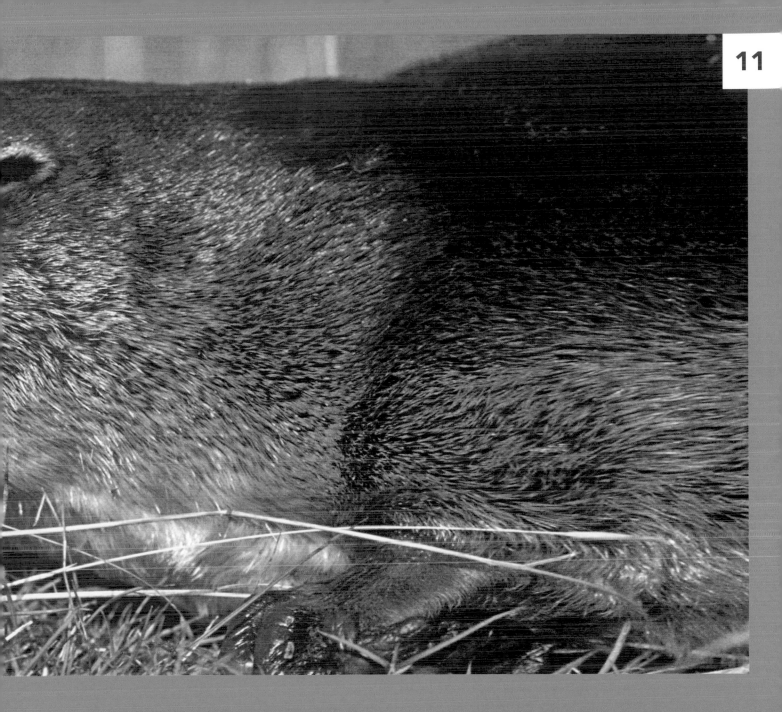

This water-dwelling mammal, which lives in Australian fresh water and estuaries, has a strange duck bill that can detect electrical activity.

Experiments have shown that its bill is sensitive to the electrical fields made by even the slightest movement of its prey. But this isn't the creature's only superpower. The platypus (meaning "bird beak") has a tail like a beaver's that it can use as a fin and as a place to store fat, for when food is scarce. This hybrid animal, like all mammals, has fur; but like a bird or reptile, lays eggs! The male platypus also has an extremely poisonous spike or "spur" on the inside of its ankle.

It's hard to categorise this animal as mammal, even though it might be the ancestor of a mammal. Instead, we've given it a separate order, *Monotremata*, which it shares with another egg-laying Australian creature: the echidna.

JUMPING SPIDER

 SUPERPOWER:
PANORAMIC SIGHT

SUPER STATS
SCIENTIFIC NAME: *Prostheclina pallida*
FAMILY: *Salticidae,* more than
5,000 species
Location: eastern Australia

SUPER FACT:
Jumping spiders such as *Prostheclina pallida* pounce on their prey.

This eight-eyed spider is worthy of a science-fiction movie!

Its eyes are elongated like an insect's, but in their structure they are more like those of a human, with a lens, jellylike liquid, light-sensitive receptors, and an optic nerve.

Unlike human eyes, this spider's eyes have several layers of retinal cells that help it judge distances and easily pinpoint prey. We don't know exactly what the jumping spider sees with its eight eyes—one picture at a time or several—but we do know that its incredible vision allows it to catch its prey by jumping on it!

COMMON OCTOPUS

🦾 **SUPERPOWER:**
SUPER INTELLIGENCE

💡 **SUPER STATS:**
SCIENTIFIC NAME: *Octopus vulgaris*
Size: 10-inch (25-centimeter) mantle;
3-feet (1-meter) tentacles
Weight: about 18 pounds (8 kilograms)
Location: worldwide

👍 **SUPER FACT:**
The octopus can unscrew the lid of a jar!

Weirdly, an octopus's brain is distributed all over its body. This super-intelligent creature can adapt to different situations and, like humans, has thoughts based on past events.

The nervous system of the octopus is made up of its brain, which is rich in cells called neurons; it has at least 500 million. These brain cells are found in a central organ in the throat; in the lobes that it uses for seeing; and in its tentacles. Because its tentacles have their own brain cells, they act as if they have a "mind" of their own.

The octopus is part of a group of invertebrates (animals without backbones) known as cephalopods. This Greek word means "head foot," and is a reference to the way the octopus's tentacles ("feet") are connected to its head.

HORSESHOE BATS

SUPERPOWER:
RADAR ECHO

SUPER STATS:
GENUS: *Rhinolophus,*
about 106 species
Habitat: caves, old houses,
churches, barns
Location: Europe, Asia, Africa
Mammal

SUPER FACT:
The horseshoe bat has
ginormous ears!

This strange-looking bat has a nose shaped like a horseshoe! Like all bats, it uses echolocation to detect its prey and avoid bumping into things.

Because they only fly at night, bats can't rely on vision for hunting. Instead, they let out high-pitched screeches—ultrasounds—that bounce off any objects around them, as well as off tasty insects. The bat's nose plays a role in sending out the ultrasounds, which come back to the bat as echos that it picks up with its huge, supersensitive ears. It's ears work just like radar antennas.

All species of bats face real difficulties today, especially from habitat loss. It's hard for them to find shelter in caves where they can peacefully sleep through the day or hibernate during the colder months. More importantly, bats are suffering from a massive reduction in insect numbers due to the toxic chemicals farmers spray on their crops to protect them.

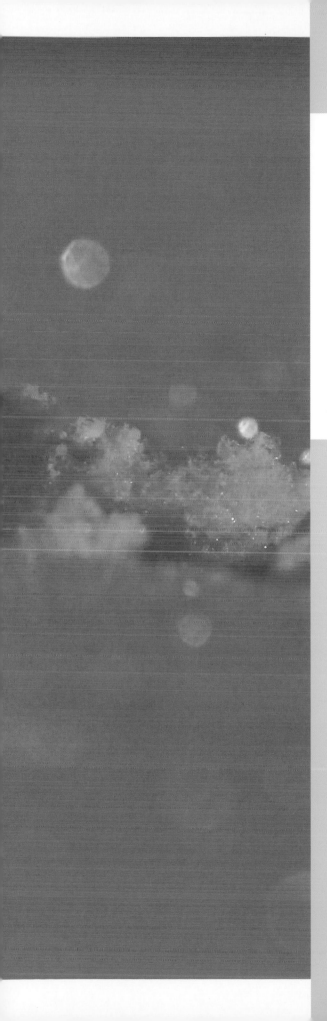

STOAT

🦾 **SUPERPOWER:**
SEASONAL TRANSFORMATION

💡 **SUPER STATS:**
SCIENTIFIC NAME: *Mustela erminea*
Size: about 9–13 inches (22–32 centimeters)
Location: worldwide
Carnivorous mammal

👍 **SUPER FACT:**
The stoat's coat changes color with the seasons.

In winter the stoat can make itself completely disappear, but how?

As winter arrives, the brown part of the stoat's coat turns white, making it almost invisible in the snow; only the black tip of its tail keeps its color. It needs this camouflage so that it can continue to prey on field mice and voles, which tunnel under the snow in winter.

The stoat is preyed on by eagle owls and mountain eagles. Having a white coat in winter helps it hide. In spring, the white fur on its back and legs is replaced by new brown fur.

During its winter phase, the stoat is often called an "ermine." Traditionally, European kings and queens used ermine fur (white with black tail tips) to trim their cloaks. Humans still hunt stoats, and in some places they are now endangered. Global warming may affect the stoat's seasonal camouflage change: what will happen when there is no snow?

METAMORPHOSIS

Imitation is an art that many species practice when they are looking for food or are trying to escape from predators. A great change in appearance or character is called a "metamorphosis."

DNA is the molecule that contains the code for all forms of life on Earth, and is passed down from parents to their offspring. Over time, DNA goes through small changes that can give rise to some extraordinary life forms. The leaf insect, for example, has adapted to look just like part of a plant, while some fish that live in schools have evolved incredible powers of illusion. We humans can't help but marvel at their gifts.

STICK AND LEAF INSECTS

 SUPERPOWER:
TOTAL INVISIBILITY

 SUPER STATS:
ORDER: *Phasmida*
3,100 species
Location: worldwide

SUPER FACT:
These insects look just like
parts of plants!

Stick and leaf insects blend in with their surroundings so well that they look just like the sticks and leaves on which they live. But why have they evolved this way?

Stick insects are peaceful vegetarians, big leaf-eaters with endless appetites. They make very appealing prey for a lot of different predators, such as birds, amphibians, and reptiles, so they need good camouflage to hide safely on the plants they eat. As their name suggests, they look just like sticks, and they even sway in the wind like twigs. Meanwhile their cousins, the leaf insects, perfectly imitate the leaves of trees, down to the finest details of color and texture, and even the network of veins. Some even have brownish edges, resembling leaves that have been nibbled by parasites, and their eggs look like little seeds!

CHAMELEONS

SUPERPOWER:
COLOR IMITATION

SUPER STATS:
FAMILY: *Chameleonidae*,
about 200 species
Size: 0.6–27 inches (1.5–70 centimeters)
Location: mostly Africa

SUPER FACT:
Their eyes can turn in different directions
at the same time!

These prankster reptiles can change color.

Chameleons have incredible powers of imitation that allow them to blend in with their surroundings. They owe this talent to special skin cells called chromatophores that contain different colored pigments, such as orange, red, brown, or yellow. Each specialized skin cell is attached to tiny muscles that can either hold the color in (by absorbing wavelengths of light) or release it. When the muscles tense up, the cells are activated and the colors appear on the chameleon's skin.

Recent studies have shown that chameleons also have tiny cells called iridophores. These contain minute crystals that, when illuminated, reflect iridescent colors, like the wings of a butterfly.

Changing color provides camouflage, but may also reflect changes in mood; help attract a mate; or help regulate body temperature.

HOVER FLIES

👍 SUPERPOWER:
PROTECTIVE DISGUISE

💡 SUPER STATS:
FAMILY: *Syrphidae*
ORDER: Diptera (flies)
SUBORDER: Brachycera
Location: almost everywhere

👍 SUPER FACT:
This fly might trick you into thinking it was a wasp.

These flies have discovered a brilliant trick: they disguise themselves as wasps so that nobody bothers them!

Biologists have given this particular method of protection a name: Batesian mimicry, after Henry Bates, the English scientist who first noticed insects performing this trick. Their disguise isn't perfect though. If you take a closer look at their wings, you'll see that they look more like the wings of flies than those of wasps or bees. Still, the illusion is good enough to put off predators who are afraid of wasp stings! It certainly works on many humans, who get scared very quickly by a wasplike insect, even if it's completely harmless.

This type of imitation is quite common in nature, particularly among reptiles such as the coral snake, and among insects, especially flies and beetles.

STARLING

 SUPERPOWER:
MAKING HOLOGRAMS IN THE SKY

SUPER STATS:
SCIENTIFIC NAME: *Sturnus vulgaris*
FAMILY: *Sturnidae*
Length: 8 inches (21 centimeters)
Wingspan: 14 inches (35 centimeters)
Slender, pointed beak; short tail; dark, speckled plumage
Migrates in some places, but not others

SUPER FACT:
A starling can copy the voice of any other bird.

Starlings gather in huge numbers so they can cast an enormous shadow and scare off predators! They gather at dusk in the place where they'll sleep. One big mass of birds means each individual is protected.

In flight, the gatherings of thousands—called a murmuration—are truly spectacular. Viewed from afar, the starlings look like a huge, shapeshifting cloud, swirling with sudden changes of direction. Any predator, such as a falcon or hawk, would be wary of attacking. Farmers dread these hungry hordes landing on their crops. Local officials don't like them either, because of the noise they make and the droppings they leave behind.

Perched at the top of a tree, a starling can copy the sounds around it. It can sing in just the same way as another bird, and can even imitate a frog!

PEACOCK BUTTERFLY

SUPERPOWER:
OPTICAL ILLUSION

SUPER STATS
SCIENTIFIC NAME: *Aglais io*
Wingspan: 2–2.5 inches
(5–6 centimeters)
Location: widespread in Europe

SUPER FACT:
The peacock butterfly's larvae
like to eat stinging nettles.

On its wings, this butterfly has four large, blue circles that look like eyes—but pay attention!

These circles are only visible when the wings are open. When its wings are closed, the butterfly is very hard to spot, camouflaged by its neutral colors. If a predator approaches, usually a bird, the butterfly opens its wings to reveal its fake eyes. A lazy predator will often be scared off, but robins and warblers, which have big appetites, may peck at the circles as if they were vicitms' heads. Despite damage to her wings, the female peacock butterfly can still go on to lay eggs on nettle leaves, which are eaten by her larvae.

The diurnal peacock butterfly has a nocturnal cousin: the great night peacock. This butterfly also has circles that look like eyes, but its colors are less vivid and it has branched antennas instead of club-shaped antennas with blobs at the end.

PANGOLINS

💪 SUPERPOWER:
FEARSOME ARMOR

💡 SUPER STATS:
FAMILY: *Manidae*
SIZE: 12–31 inches (30–80 centimeters)
Habitat: tropical and equatorial regions in Africa and Southeast Asia

👍 SUPER FACT:
Pangolins are the only mammals that are completely covered in scales.

A pangolin is covered in large, tough scales. These make an impressive suit of armor for its body and tail, protecting them from even the sharpest teeth, beaks, or claws of predators.

Pangolins occupy a huge range, from Africa to Southeast Asia. They are peaceful, insect-eating animals with mostly nocturnal habits. Their sticky tongues are unusually good at catching large numbers of termites and ants. If attacked, they tighten up their scales and curl into a ball, protecting the more delicate parts of their bodies.

Regrettably, the pangolin's most dangerous predator is humans. Although a protected species in most countries, it is prized by some people for its meat and is also poached for its scales, which are used to combat allergies. Two of the eight pangolin species are listed as critically endangered with extinction.

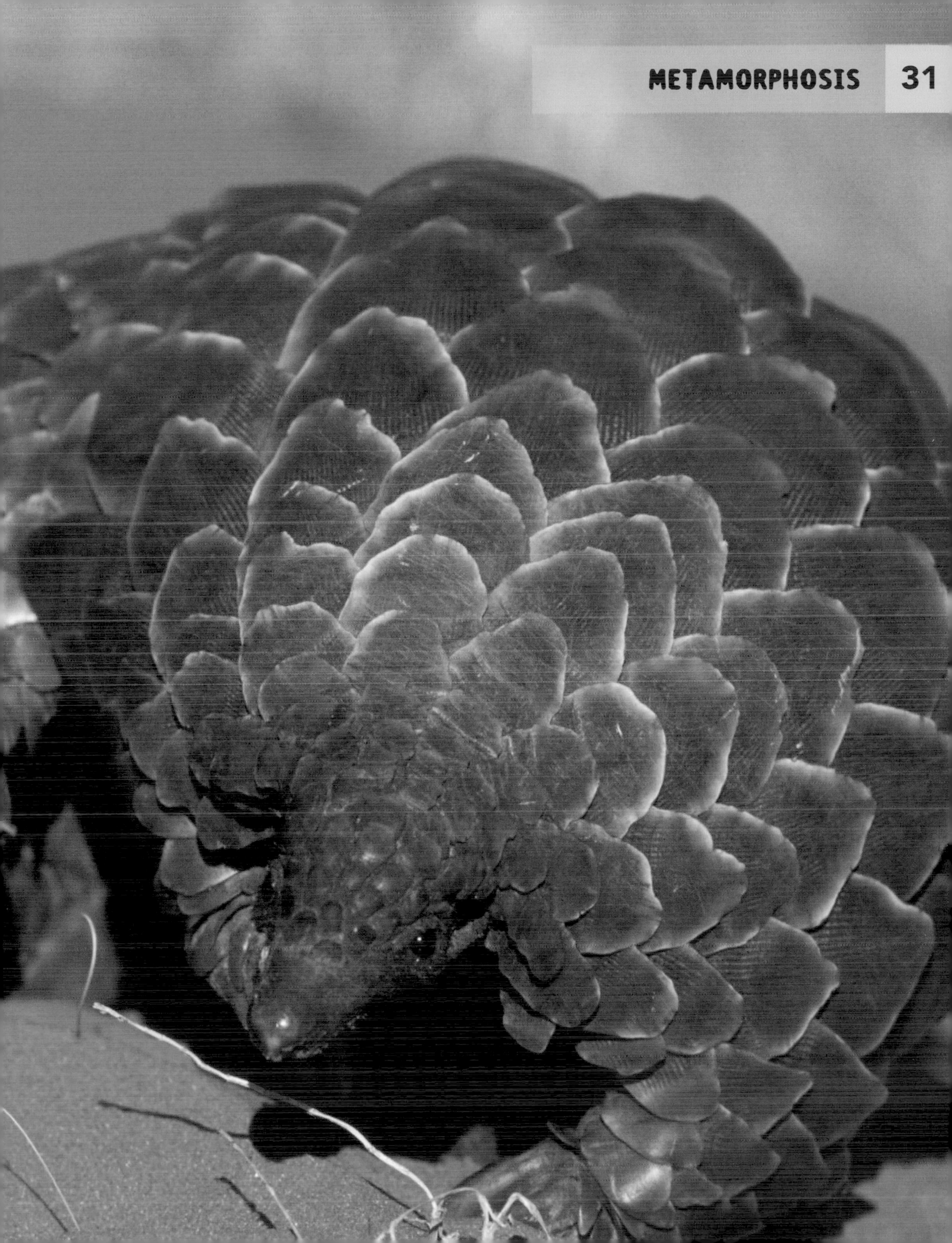

STRAWBERRY POISON-DART FROG

SUPERPOWER:
POWERFUL REPELLING

SUPER STATS:
SCIENTIFIC NAME:
Dendrobates pumilio
Size 0.7–0.9 inch
(1.7–2.4 centimeters)
Location: Central America

SUPER FACT:
A very toxic frog that mimics even more toxic frogs!

What's the opposite of camouflage? Showing yourself off as much as possible, so as not to be eaten!

In their tropical rainforest home, tiny red, blue, and orange strawberry poison-dart frogs are eaten by…no-one! Absolutely no predator will attack them. Their bright colors act as a warning sign: "Watch out, I taste terrible!" Their colors mimic other brightly colored frogs that are even more poisonous than they are. Any predator

that tries to eat these other frogs ends up wretching violently, so it learns to avoid anything resembling the most toxic species, including the strawberry poison-dart frog. Biologists call this kind of reverse camouflage "Müllerian mimicry," named for Franz Müller, a German zoologist.

Some mushrooms, such as the bright red-and-white fly agaric, also exhibit bright colors to warn off predators. The colors advertise them as being extremely toxic.

PUSS MOTH CATERPILLAR

SUPERPOWER:
SCARY MASK

SUPER STATS:
SCIENTIFIC NAME:
Cerura vinula
ORDER: Lepidoptera
Habitat: damp places, often near water

SUPER FACT:
This creature can squirt acid a distance of up to 4 inches (10 centimeters)!

The puss moth caterpillar has a mask around its face to scare away hungry predators. It generally works for birds that are not very brave!

The caterpillar draws in the segments at the front of its body to reveal its red, puffy face. Around its face is a bright pink ring with two false eyes at the top. The false eyes fool predators into thinking the caterpillar is a larger creature than it really is. From its tail end, it extends two long whips, which it waves furiously at anything threatening. It can also squirt a jet of formic acid a distance of 4 inches (10 centimeters).

The puss moth caterpillar lives in damp woodland, feeding on the leaves of willow and poplar trees. Eventually it turns into a large, fluffy moth decorated with black zigzags.

SKILLED MOVERS

You might think that all animals can move from place to place, but that's not actually the case. Some animals that live in the ocean are fixed in one spot and can't travel at all. At the opposite end of the spectrum are animals that have developed incredible powers of mobility, such as cheetahs, peregrine falcons, and flying squirrels. Over time, these species have evolved great powers of movement, linked to their roles as predators. Whether catching prey or escaping predators themselves, they can move amazingly quickly.

PEREGRINE FALCON

 SUPERPOWER:
AS FAST AS A HIGH-SPEED TRAIN

SUPER STATS:
SCIENTIFIC NAME: *Falco peregrinus*
Wingspan: 29–47 inches
(74–120 centimeters)

SUPER FACT:
After almost dying out in the 1960s,
poisoned by chemicals on crops, peregrine
falcons are increasing in number.

**The peregrine falcon can swoop down on
its prey at 200 miles per hour, making it the
fastest bird—and animal—in the world!**

As soon as it spies a starling, pigeon, or jackdaw,
it soars upward, works out the correct angle, then
plunges down with its wings tight against its body.
This rocketlike bird will fly beneath a flock of birds,
re-angle itself, then drive straight at its unfortunate
victim, often a younger or injured bird trailing
behind the rest of the flock. Then it carries its prey
back to its favorite rock and it devours it, leaving
only the carcass.

Peregrine falcons typically live on rocky cliffs, both
inland and on the coast. They are now also found
living in towns and cities, nesting on church towers
and other tall buildings, which provide great
lookouts for prey below.

FLYING SQUIRREL

 SUPERPOWER:
FLYING WITHOUT WINGS

 SUPER STATS:
SCIENTIFIC NAME: *Glaucomys volans*
Location: North America
Generally nocturnal

SUPER FACT:
The flying squirrel has giant eyes
for seeing in the dark.

Imagine this: a squirrel soaring between two trees! This may sound surprising, but it is an everyday thing for flying squirrels.

These North American rodents glide from tree to tree thanks to a furry membrane, called a patagium, stretched between their front and back legs.

At night, this furry mammal clambers to the top of a tree to feed. Then it launches itself into the air and glides to the next tree. A flying squirrel can only glide downward; if it launches from high enough, it can glide for tens of feet. The patagium acts like a parachute, which it adjusts by moving its legs. When it wants to land, it flattens out its body to get maximum air resistance. This dazzling technique inspired the invention of the wingsuit, a webbing-sleeved jumpsuit worn by some skydivers.

CHEETAH

 SUPERPOWER:
RECORD-HOLDING
ACCELERATION

SUPER STATS:
SCIENTIFIC NAME:
Acinonyx jubatus
FAMILY: *Felidae*
Appearance: coat spotted
with black "tears"
Location: Africa

 SUPER FACT:
A cheetah can accelerate
from 0 to 60 miles per
hour in three seconds—
faster than most
automobiles!

The cheetah's superpower is speed; it is the fastest land animal in the world, with a top speed of 70 miles per hour!

However, it can only maintain this speed for short distances; if it wants to eat, it has to catch its prey very quickly and kill it on the spot. With its keen eyesight, the cheetah picks out an impala, gazelle, or young wildebeest to chase. Once it has spotted its target, it approaches slowly through the long grasses of the savanna. Then, it accelerates at incredible speed and pounces on its prey. If it doesn't bring down the animal first time around, its prey is likely to escape.

The cheetah is part of the *Felidae* family, along with cats, lions, and leopards. Its distinctive features are its slender body and non-retractable claws, which act like the spikes on a sprinter's shoes. Sadly, this marvel of nature is in great danger. In the big parks of southern and eastern Africa where it now lives, vehicles of tourists disrupt the cheetah's hunting routine.

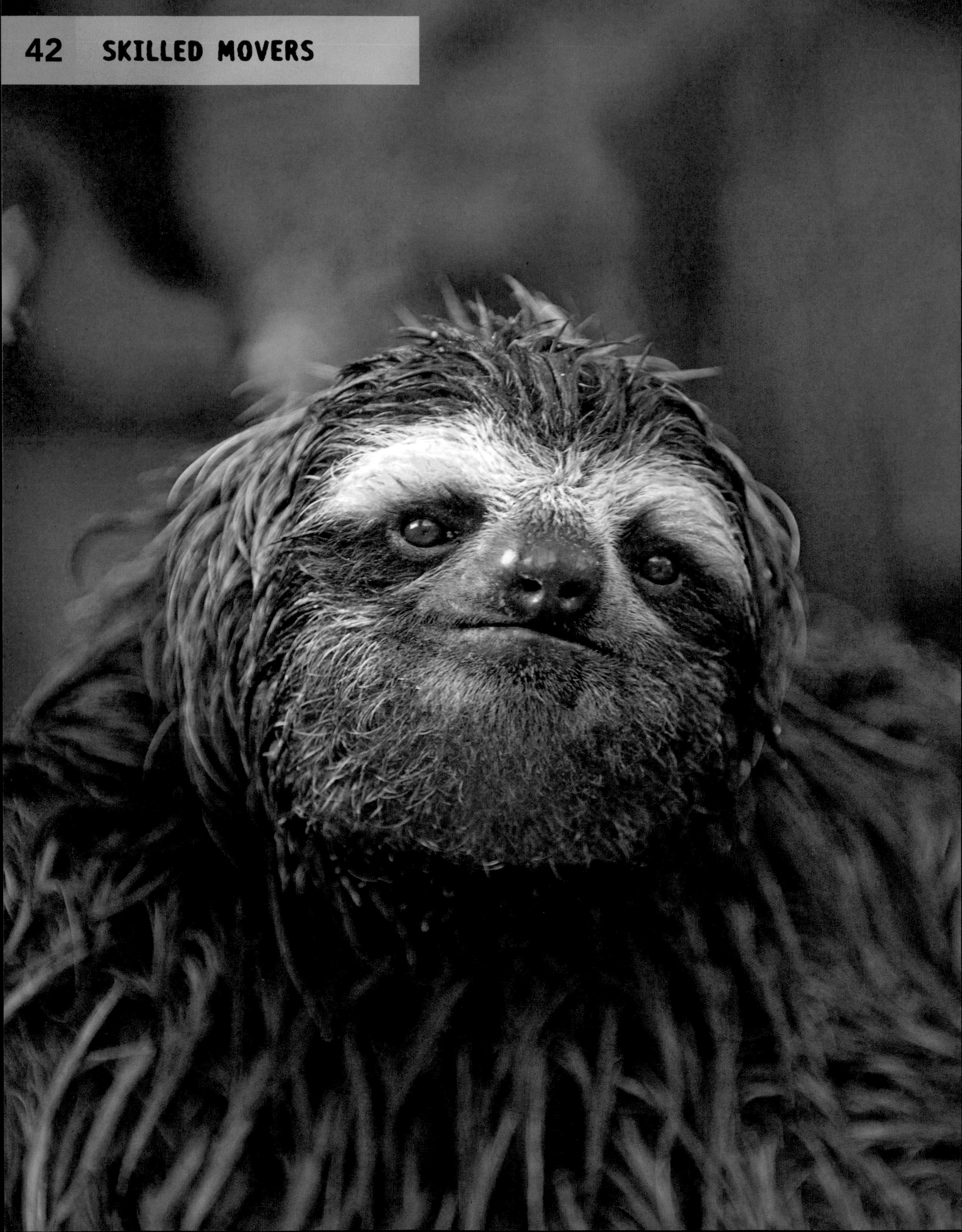

SLOTHS

SUPERPOWER:
EXTREMELY SLOW MOTION

SUPER STATS:
SUBORDER: Folivora
Size: 24–33 inches
(60–85 centimeters)
Herbivorous mammals
Habitat: tropical forests
Location: Central/South America

SUPER FACT:
Using its powerful claws, it can
hang upside down all week long!

**Sloths not only move very slowly; they
poop very slowly, too!**

A sloth mostly eats tough leaves, which it digests
over the course of more than a week. It then
descends from its tree very slowly and does its
business on the forest floor, relieving itself of a
third of its body weight! The slowness with which
it moves, together with its greenish-brown coat,
help it go unnoticed by predators. The green
flecks on its fur are bacteria and algae.

Depending on the species, some sloths have
two fingers on each limb; others have three. The
fingers are armed with powerful hooked claws
that it uses to hang upside down from branches.

Unusually, a sloth's neck is made from eight parts,
and this allows it to rotate its head almost the
whole way around!

SWIFT

SUPERPOWER:
UNBREAKABLE ENDURANCE

SUPER STATS:
SCIENTIFIC NAME: *Apus apus*
Wingspan: 18 inches (45 centimeters)
Insectivore
Migrates

SUPER FACT:
This bird never stops flying!

The swift hardly ever lands! It can eat insects in flight, sleep in the sky, and even mate in the air.

Swifts and swallows are often confused because they look similar from afar, but they belong to separate families. Swifts belong to the *Apodidae* family, which means "having no feet," but this description is not strictly true! Swifts do have feet, but they are only small because it has little need of them. The only time it uses its feet is when it clambers under roofs to make its nest from material it has caught in flight. It then lays its eggs and cares for the chicks. When the young are ready to fledge the nest in August, they throw themselves into the air and fly away, only returning the following July, when it's their turn to mate.

Swifts are migratory birds. In August, they head for Africa, because there aren't many insects to eat in Europe in fall and winter. They return every year on exactly the same date, give or take only one or two days, unless a storm or a cold snap forces them to delay their trip.

PLUMED BASILISK

 **SUPERPOWER:**
RUNNING ON
WATER

 SUPER STATS:
SCIENTIFIC NAME:
Basiliscus plumifrons
Length: 31 inches
(80 centimeters)
Habitat: tropical forests
Location: Central/South America

SUPER FACT:
Amazingly, this lizard
can scamper across the
surface of water!

The plumed basilisk will run for its life across water to escape from predators such as snakes and opossums!

For a short distance it can run across water by taking big strides on its two back legs. Its two long arms barely sink below the surface. Two things help prevent it from sinking: it maintains a speed of more than 6 miles per hour and it weighs just 7 ounces (200 grams). With its helmeted head and long dorsal crest, inherited from distant reptilian ancestors, the basilisk looks like a little dragon. Indeed, it is named for a dragon from ancient Greek myth that could turn people to stone just by looking at them. The basilisk's nickname is the "Jesus Christ Lizard," from the Bible story that tells us Jesus "walked on water." In its tropical forest home, its emerald-green body makes it hard to spot. It hides in trees and makes its escape by sliding down the trunks. As well as insects, it eats spiders, mammals, birds, fruit, and leaves.

HUMMINGBIRDS

SUPERPOWER:
FLYING BACKWARD

SUPER STATS:
FAMILY: *Trochilidae,*
340 species
Size: 2–8 inches (5–20 centimeters)
Weight: 0.07–0.7 ounce (2–20 grams)

SUPER FACT:
Hummingbirds can hover in mid-flight, and can even fly backward—something other birds cannot do.

By vibrating its muscles at high speed, in just one second a hummingbird can beat its wings up to 70 times!

This superpower allows it to hover while it drinks nectar from flowers, and even fly backward to get the best angle or to make way for more aggressive species. The hummingbird feeds by inserting its extendable forked tongue into the centers of flowers, even ones with very deep heads. As it feeds, pollen grains from the flower stick to the hummingbird's bill and feathers. When the bird visits the next flower, some of the pollen is transferred. If both flowers are the same species, pollination occurs. These birds do the same job of fertilizing plants in the tropics as insects, especially bees, do in Europe. Because they do this job, bee hummingbirds are almost all very small. The smallest species of hummingbird weighs just 0.07 ounce (2 grams)!

GECKOS

 **SUPERPOWER:**
WALKING ON THE
CEILING

 SUPER STATS:
FAMILY: *Gekkonidae*
Reptile
Location: all hot or temperate
regions
Habitat: humid places
Life expectancy: 13–20 years

SUPER FACT:
Geckos use microscopic
hairs to cling to surfaces.

The gecko has a gravity-defying grip!

This small lizard likes to get into homes and take up residence on the walls or ceilings, where it will snap up any insects that land nearby.

Although it weighs only about 1.8 ounces (50 grams), the gecko can resist 4.4 pounds (2 kilograms) of pulling force by gripping the surface it's on. Amazingly, despite its grip, it can still move at very high speed. Each finger—five per foot—is lined with microscopic hairs that end in even smaller structures called "spatula." The molecules of the spatula are strongly attracted to the molecules of the surface the gecko is on, so temporarily they can't be pulled apart. Physicists call these "Van Der Waals" forces. If it wants to travel, the gecko turns its legs very slightly, which releases its feet. Researchers today are trying to artificially recreate this mechanism to make a powerful type of Scotch tape!

SQUID

SUPERPOWER:
JET PROPULSION

SUPER STATS:
ORDER: Teuthida
Size: about 2–20 feet (0.6–6 meters)
Location: worldwide
Habitat: oceans and seas, both warm and cold

SUPER FACT:
Squid have two extra-long tentacles that shoot out to capture prey.

A squid is a water-dwelling mollusk that moves backward through the water using jet propulsion, a useful skill when there's an enemy in sight.

Like their cuttlefish cousins, squid have many sea predators, such as sperm whales and dolphins. Fishermen also trap tons of squid in their nets. Cuttlefish, octopuses, and squid are all cephalopods (meaning "head foot" in Greek); they all have tentacles around their heads. A squid moves by sucking water into its funnel-like body and quickly shooting it out through a narrow siphon, sending itself backward. When danger threatens, it expels a jet of black ink into the water that forms a cloud, hiding it from view.

Many squid are small, slim animals, but the giant squid and the colossal squid can both grow to more than 39 feet (12 meters) in length, making them the world's largest invertebrates.

SUPER ADAPTERS

Animals live everywhere on Earth, even in places with the most extreme conditions. How are they able to survive? The answer is "adaptations!"

Adaptations are characteristics that help an animal survive in its habitat. Animals have adapted in ways that put human abilities to shame. Bacteria, for example, can thrive in environments that are much too hot or too cold for people. While humans can't live without light, some creatures can live in total darkness. The tiny tardigrade can even withstand practically any kind of trauma. It seems that the power of animal life has no limits, other than those we humans impose.

CLOWNFISH

🦾 **SUPERPOWER:**
RESISTANCE TO POISON

⬡ **SUPER STATS:**
SCIENTIFIC NAME: *Amphiprion ocellaris*
FAMILY: *Pomacentridae*
Size: 2.4–6 inches (6–16 centimeters)
Lifespan: 6–10 years
Location: warm, shallow parts of the Indian and Pacific oceans and the Red Sea

👍 **SUPER FACT:**
The most famous clownfish is the orange-and-white striped cartoon fish, Nemo!

An adult clownfish spends its whole life between an anemone's poisonous tentacles!

Clownfish live in the warm waters of sheltered reefs and lagoons. While still young, the clownfish will adopt a sea anemone, and stay with it for the rest of its life. The relationship is symbiotic, meaning each party helps the other out. The anemone has stinging cells, called cnidocysts, that put off any predator attracted to the clownfish's bright colors. In return, the clownfish cleans out any bits of food that get stuck between the anemone's tentacles. Why does the clownfish not get stung by the anemone's poisonous cells? It is protected by a thick layer of mucus that covers its scales, allowing it to dive safely between the anemone's tentacles if danger approaches.

EM. E...U... PENGUIN

💪 **SUPERPOWER:**
TEMPERATURE REGULATION

💡 **SUPER STATS:**
SCIENTIFIC NAME: *Aptenodytes forsteri*
FAMILY: *Spheniscidae*
Height: approx. 3.3 feet (1 meter)
Weight: 44–88 pounds (20–40 kilograms)
Location: Antarctica and surrounding islands

👍 **SUPER FACT:**
These community-minded penguins keep each other warm.

Even when it's -58 degrees Fahrenheit (-50 degrees Celsius), the emperor penguin can keep its internal temperature at 100.4 degrees Fahrenheit (38 degrees Celsius)!

Living in colonies on floating platforms of ice in Antarctica, these penguins are optimized to avoid losing heat: nothing on their bodies sticks out, and their flipperlike wings and tails are very short. They have four layers of feathers, a thick layer of fat, and a special circulatory system that keeps them warm when temperatures are very low. The warm blood in their arteries goes to their feet, where it cools on contact with nearby veins before warming again on the way back up. In blizzard conditions, the penguins huddle in a tight circle. At intervals, those on the inside take the place of those more exposed to the cold on the outer edge of the circle.

AXOLOTL

 SUPERPOWER:
SELF-REGENERATION

SUPER STATS:
SCIENTIFIC NAME: *Ambystoma mexicanum*
Length: 10 inches (25 centimeters)
Habitat: fresh water
Location: Mexico
Critically endangered species

SUPER FACT:
This little creature never grows up!

A lizard may be able to regrow its tail, but the axolotl can regenerate any part of its body!

However, the axolotl isn't a reptile, like a lizard; it's an amphibian, like a salamander. This very rare creature lives only in a few caves and lakes in Mexico. If it loses a limb in a fight with a predator, in just a few days it can grow a new one. Scientists have even successfully experimented with making one axolotl out of two, joining together the body of one and the head of another.

The axolotl's amazing ability to regenerate is linked to something called "neoteny:" the delaying or slowing of physical development. In other words, the axolotl stays in its larval form for its whole life, never growing up into an adult (imagine a frog staying a tadpole forever). As well as retaining the gills of the larval form, it also holds on to the powers of an embryo, the unborn or undeveloped form of a species. The cells of an embryo have the capacity to turn into any organ. Hence the axolotl can regrow its limbs.

HEDGEHOG

SUPERPOWER:
LIVING IN THE SLOW LANE

SUPER STATS
SCIENTIFIC NAME: *Erinaceus europaeus*
Weight: 28 ounces (800 grams)
Nocturnal, omnivorous mammal
Hibernates in winter

SUPER FACT:
When hibernating, its heartbeat drops from 300 to 5 beats per minute!

When winter approaches, the hedgehog books itself a long vacation!

All it needs is a cosy place to settle down: a hollow between tree roots, a pile of wood, or a few dead leaves for a bed. Then it curls up into a ball, ready to sleep for several months.

The onset of cold weather triggers some dramatic changes in this little creature: its heart rate, usually 200–300 beats per minute, slows to less than 10; and its body temperature plummets from 100 degrees Fahrenheit to just 39.2 (38 to 4 degrees Celsius). Part of its energy-saving strategy involves keeping movement to a minimum, reducing heat exchange, and reducing bodily functions to their most basic form. Come the spring, the hedgehog's heartbeat and temperature return to normal.

TARDIGRADES

SUPERPOWER:
INDESTRUCTIBILITY

SUPER STATS
PHYLUM: Tardigrada,
more than 1,200 species
Size: 0.004–0.06 inch
(0.1–1.5 millimeters)
Common names: water
bear; moss piglet

SUPER FACT:
You might find a
tardigrade surviving
on top of a Himalayan
mountain or 13,100 feet
(4,000 meters) deep
in the ocean.

These miniscule eight-legged invertebrates armed with claws are completely indestructible!

Their normal living conditions would be fatal to most other organisms. Tardigrades can easily stand extreme heat as well as intense cold. After a long stay in the freezer—as long as thirty years—a tardigrade can wake up with no problem. Similarly, it can emerge from boiling water and be back to its usual business in a matter of minutes. In a 2007 experiement,

tardigrades even managed to survive in the vacuum of outer space; back on Earth, they showed no signs of damage. Their truly incredible toughness is attributed to a specific protein in their bodies that helps to repair their DNA when it's broken down by extreme conditions. When enduring harsh conditions, a tardigrade switches into a mode even slower than hibernation. Barely breathing at all, its body almost completely dehydrates. Although they are too small to spot, they live all around us, especially in mosses, soil, dunes, and mud.

DROMEDARY

SUPERPOWER:
GOING WITHOUT
WATER

SUPER STATS:
SCIENTIFIC NAME:
Camelus dromedarius
FAMILY: *Camelidae*
Height: 6.5 feet (2 meters)
Weight: 1,100 pounds
(500 kilograms)

SUPER FACT:
The most common camel
species, the dromedary,
has just one hump.

The dromedary, like its Bactrian-camel cousins, can survive for months in the desert without a drop of water!

Its entire bodily system is geared toward this feat: since it doesn't sweat, it loses practically no water to the outside world; it's pee is super-concentrated (lots of waste, very little water); and its droppings are almost dry. In addition, it keeps a store of fat in its hump. When the fat cells break down, water molecules are channeled straight into the dromedary's bloodstream. If not hydrated, the hump gets gradually smaller until it just hangs sadly to one side. When the dromedary drinks again, the hump rehydrates super-quickly, absorbing many gallons of water in a few minutes.

Desert mice are even better than camels at surviving without water. They don't drink anything at all, making do with the morning dew and the slight humidity of their burrows.

FLATFISH

**In adulthood, a flatfish's two eyes move
over to the same side of its head!**

At the earliest stage of development, a flatfish's
eyes are located on either side of its
head, and the young fish look quite
similar to other kinds of fish. As it
grows to adulthood, however,
it undergoes a change. The
flatfish's vertical body tilts to
become horizontal, and one of its
two eyes moves over to be closer
to the other eye, on the top side of
its body.

The flat bodies of these fish are adapted to
live on the sandy seabed, where the fish stay
completely still for most of the day. Having
both eyes on top of their head helps them
catch small prey and spot predators. If they
sense danger, the fish writhe around on the
seabed, creating clouds of sand that shield
them from view. They become practically
invisible, apart from their beady eyes.

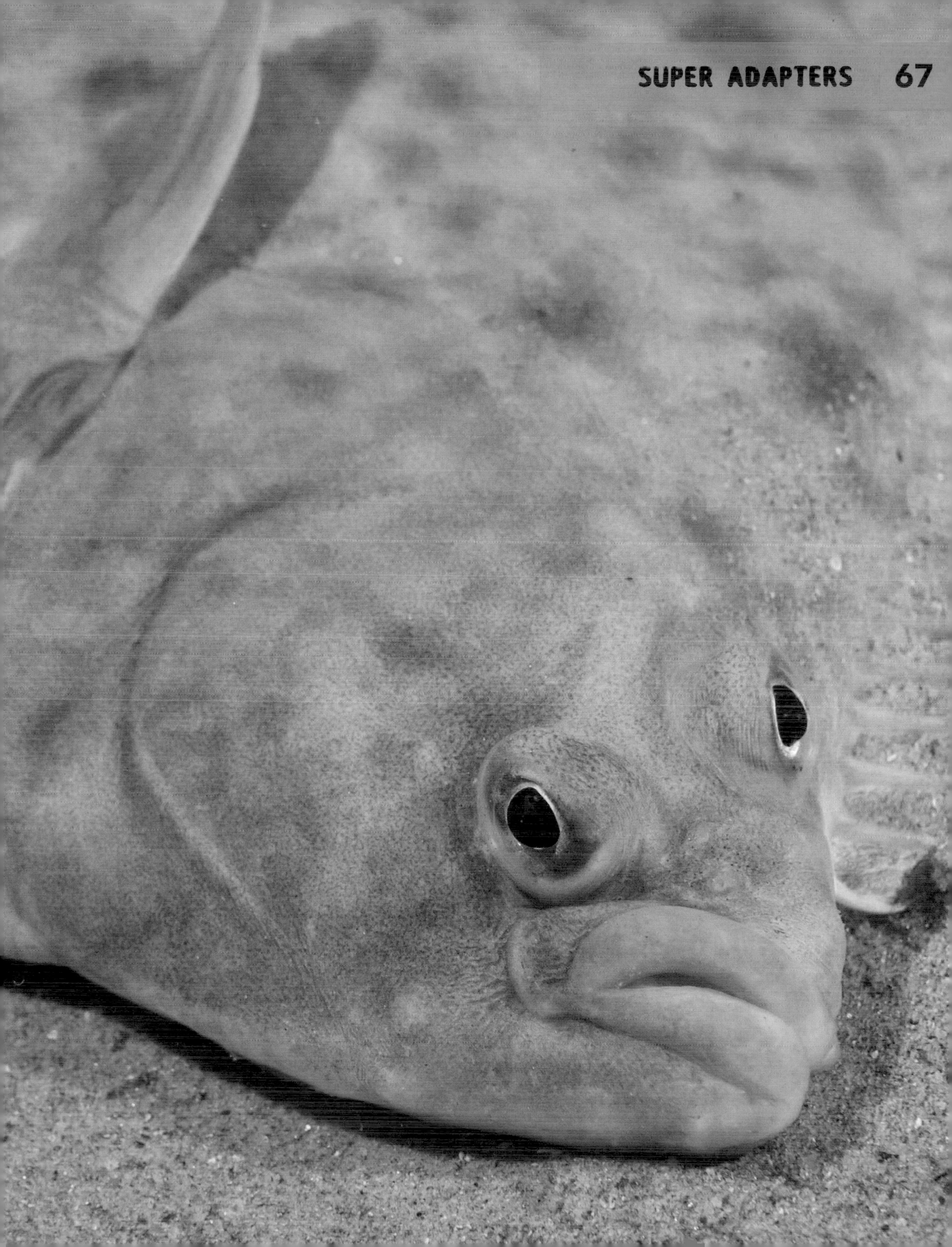

WOOD FROG

 SUPERPOWER:
ANTIFREEZE

 SUPER STATS:
SCIENTIFIC NAME: *Rana sylvatica*
Size: 2–2.7 inches (5–7 centimeters)
Location: USA (including Alaska) and Canada

SUPER FACT:
In the most extreme cold, this frog partially freezes, but lives to tell the tale!

This frog can freeze and unfreeze itself without upsetting its bodily functions!

When temperatures plummet in the North American forests where it lives, including some north of the Arctic Circle, the wood frog's liver makes lots of the sugar molecules called glucose. This glucose spreads throughout its blood as it enters its sluggish winter phase. The high level of glucose lowers the frog's internal freezing point, stopping the fluids inside it from turning to ice. While the temperature is below freezing, its major bodily functions (breathing, heartbeat, kidneys) slow almost to a standstill.

When spring approaches, the wood frog's metabolism gradually picks up again. As soon as the temperature rises, its vital functions rediscover their rhythm, and the frog gets back to its favorite activity —feeding itself!

MARY RIVER TURTLE

SUPERPOWER:
BUTT-BREATHING

SUPER STATS:
SCIENTIFIC NAME: *Elusor macrurus*
Habitat: Fresh water
Location: Queensland, Australia
Endangered species

SUPER FACT:
Because it can breathe using special glands in its reproductive organs, the Mary River turtle can survive underwater for up to three days!

Colorful algae sprout from this strange turtle's head, giving rise to its nickname: "punk turtle!"

While it mostly breathes through its wide nostrils, this Australian freshwater turtle also has another kind of breathing system that allows it to stay underwater for up to 72 hours. It extracts oxygen from the water through gill-like structures in its "cloaca"—basically its butt!

This turtle is found only in Queensland, Australia, specifically in a single river: the Mary River. Sadly, this rare species is threatened with extinction. Having been captured for years and sold into the reckless pet trade, it's now seeing its natural habitat shrink due to the building of dams.

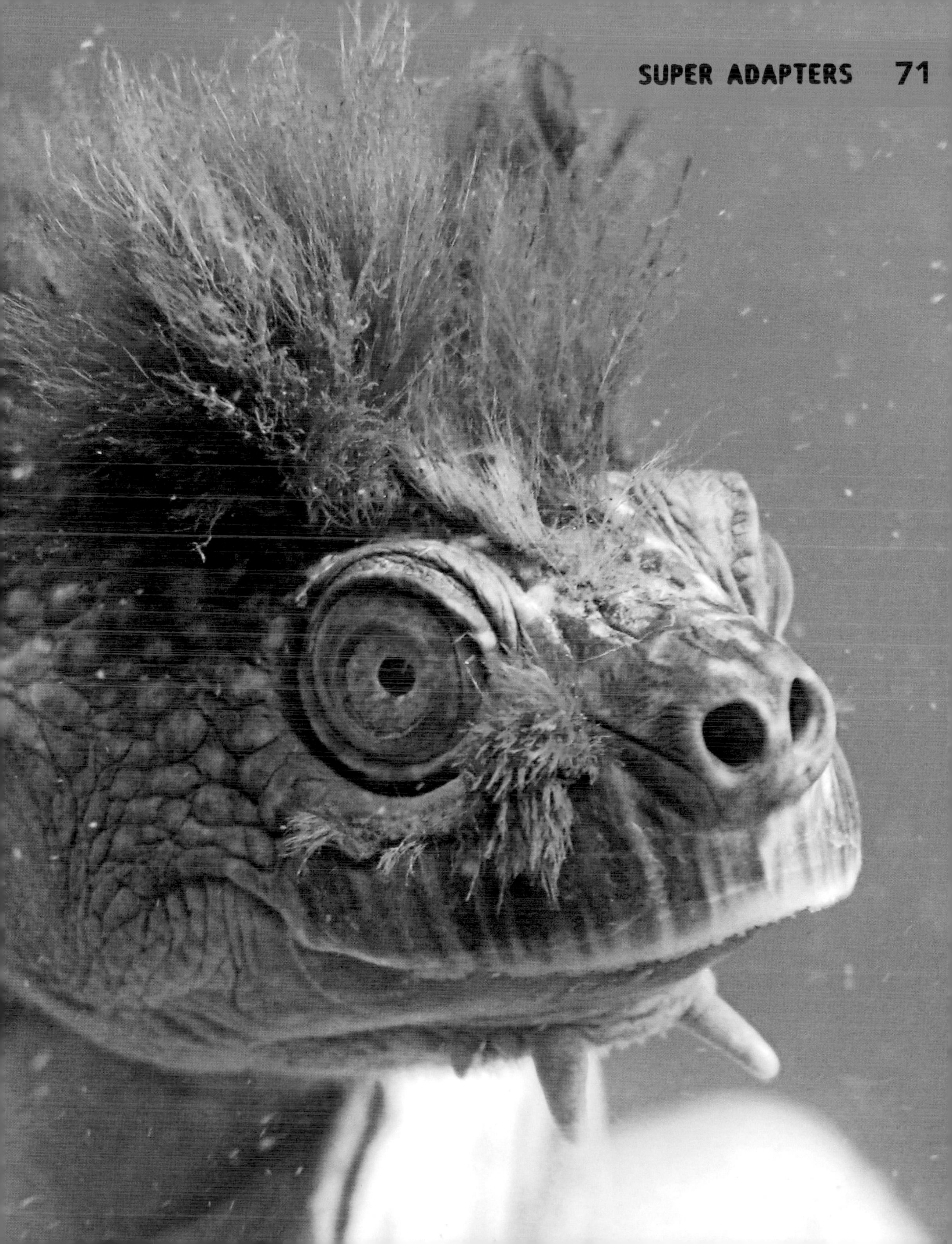

ATTRACTING A MATE

For a species to continue, it has to reproduce.

Lots of plants and some animals do this through something called "natural cloning," where an individual's DNA is copied identically to make a "child." But the other kind of reproduction, known as "sexual reproduction," plays an important role in evolution. From one female parent and one male parent, a unique child is born! Over time, animals have come up with more and more incredible strategies to make sure this happens; new ways of attracting partners and new ways of mating. The male stag beetle physically fights off any rivals; the satin bowerbird builds an attractive nest. It's a constant carnival, a song and dance!

CUCKOO

SUPERPOWER:
IDENTITY THEFT

SUPER STATS:
SCIENTIFIC NAME: *Cuculus canorus*
Wingspan: 22–26 inches (55–65 centimeters)
Life-expectancy: about 13 years

SUPER FACT:
The name "cuckoo" imitates the distinctive call of the male bird in spring.

The female cuckoo lays her egg in a nest belonging to another bird. First she chooses a nest that looks well laid out; then she lays her egg there.

The nest the female chooses normally belongs to a small bird such as a robin, sparrow, or reed warbler. Weirdly, the cuckoo egg takes on the color of the other eggs in the nest. The cuckoo egg hatches first, and the chick, with a great deal of effort, then uses its back to push out of the nest as many of the host bird's eggs as it can. The adoptive parents then feed the cuckoo chick as if it were their own, until it very quickly grows too big for the nest. The young cuckoo finally leaves, having made good use of this "hotel," and flies off to Africa to spend the winter there.

You wouldn't think a cuckoo would be so mischievous when you hear it announcing the spring with its warbling call: "cuckoo! cuckoo!"

SATIN BOWERBIRDS

 SUPERPOWER:
MAKING HIMSELF
LOOK BIGGER!

SUPER STATS:
FAMILY: *Ptilonorhynchidae*
Size: 10–12.5 inches
(25–32 centimeters)
Weight: 7 ounces (200 grams)
Location: Northeast Queensland
and Southeast Australia

SUPER FACT:
The bowerbird is a
resourceful interior
decorator.

When the male of this Australian species wants to attract a lady, he rolls out a fabulous "red carpet."

During the mating season in the month of May, the male bowerbird gets very excited. To make himself stand out from other males and be noticed by a female, he gathers a load of long twigs and branches and weaves them into an elaborate entryway to his living space. But that's not all! He also decorates the path with little pebbles, shells, fossils, fruits, flowers, feathers, and whatever bits of fabric and plastic he can find. As the female approaches, the male struts and dances, and throws his little objects around. If the courting ritual is a success, the blue-eyed female will enter the tunnel and approach him. Framed by the tunnel, from the female's viewpoint the male looks bigger; an optical illusion designed to make him more alluring to her. Truly, the bowerbird is an artistic genius!

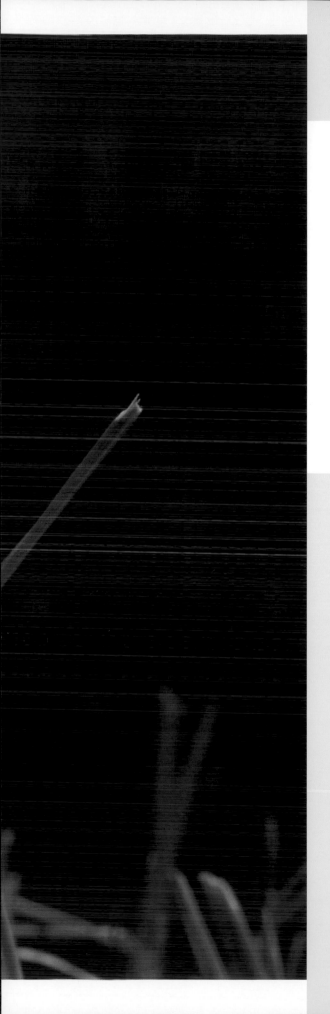

FIREFLIES

🦾 **SUPERPOWER:**
CHARMING LIGHT-GIVER

💡 **SUPER STATS:**
FAMILY: *Lampyridae*
Average lifespan: about 2 months
Size: up to 1 inch (2.5 centimeters)
Location: temperate and tropical regions,
but highly endangered

👍 **SUPER FACT:**
The *Lampyridae* family includes more than
2,000 species of light-producing beetles.

The firefly can make its own light! It's hard to imagine a superpower more exciting than being able to light a built-in lantern in the dark of night. This is the gift of fireflies and glowworms.

In the case of glowworms—mis-named, as they're actually a type of beetle—the female makes a green light glow in her abdomen to attract males. Fireflies, which belong to the same family of beetles, also shine a beautiful light from their abdomens when they're in flight. This light production is the result of a chemical reaction.

The overuse of toxic chemicals—pesticides, herbicides, and insecticides—on farmland threatens the survival of these amazing creatures. Light pollution is also a problem for them, along with firefly tourism. Firefly populations are thought to be declining worldwide. Conservationists are seeking ways to protect these splendid insects, emblems of nature's incredible biochemical diversity.

SALMON

 SUPERPOWER:
INTREPID
TRAVELING

SUPER STATS:
FAMILY: *Salmomonidae*
Maximum size: 59 inches
(150 centimeters), males
Maximum weight: 55 pounds
(25 kilograms)
Location: northern hemisphere

SUPER FACT:
The salmon goes through
multiple transformations
in its life.

The salmon has an amazing sense of smell; it can detect just a few scent molecules among millions of other smells.

What does it use this amazing superpower for? From way out in the ocean, the salmon uses its sense of smell to find its way back to the freshwater stream where it was born, so it can lay its own eggs there. The eggs hatch in the freshwater stream, and the babies, called fry, stay there for up to three years. As young adults, or smolt, they move downstream and transform from freshwater to seawater fish. Then they swim out into the open ocean, where they spend most of their adult lives. When it's time to reproduce, they set off on an epic journey back to their birthplace. While smell is their main guide, they can also make out ancient paths imprinted in the seabed that show where rivers used to flow when the sea level was lower. The salmon now turn back into freshwater fish and swim upriver to the same freshwater stream where they were born.

STAG BEETLE

 SUPERPOWER:
SUPER STRENGTH

 SUPER STATS:
SCIENTIFIC NAME: *Lucanus cervus*
Size: up to 4 inches (10 centimeters)
Location: Europe
Almost endangered

SUPER FACT:
Stag beetles can be powerful fighters.

This large beetle can lift up to 200 times its own weight, the equivalent of a 154-pound (70-kilogram) man lifting 10 cars!

The stag beetle is the most formidable of all European insects. The male is an impressive 4 inches (10 centimeters) long. It has two enormous jaws called mandibles that look like the antlers of a stag, giving this beetle its name. You might think it would use these jaws for eating; but during its short life it actually eats very little other than a few plants. Instead, its oversized pincers are used as weapons, and for attracting females, who have much smaller mandibles.

In their epic fights over females, pincer against pincer, one male will lift up another to get him to leave the scene. There are normally no casualties in these incredible fights, only a rejected suitor!

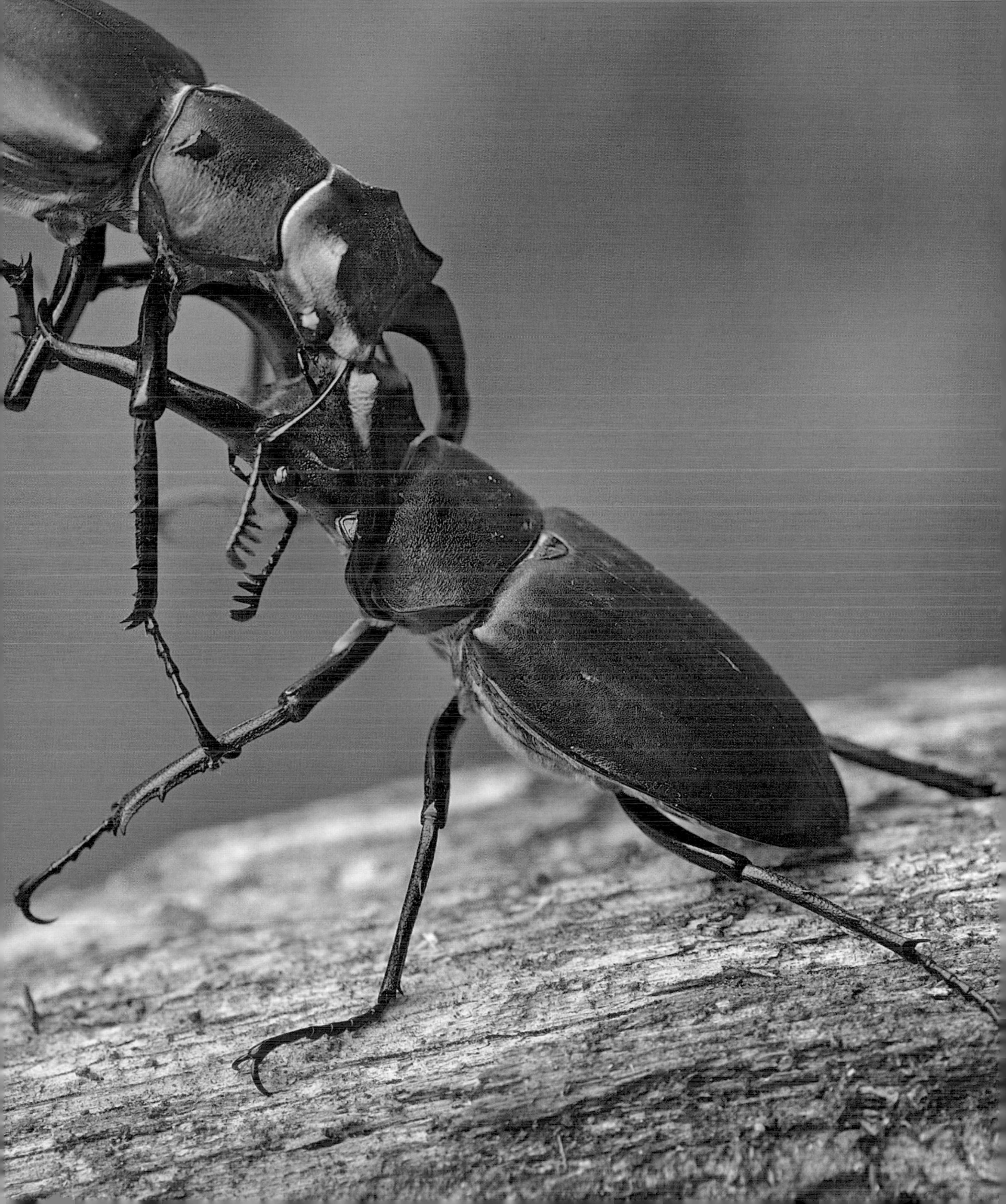

HUNTING POWER

To make your body work, you need to give it the fuel it needs for producing energy and building new cells. This process is called "nutrician."

Plants have a big advantage here, since they can survive just by taking carbon from the air, water and minerals from soil, and light and energy from the sun.

Animals can't fuel their bodies this way; to gain the nutrients they need to produce energy, they must either eat organic matter in the form of vegetables or leaves, or they must hunt and eat other animals.

This chapter looks at some of the incredible hunting techniques that animals such as the archer fish and pelican have developed so they can fuel their bodies for survival.

WOODPECKERS

 SUPERPOWER:
BEAK LIKE A HAMMER

SUPER STATS:
FAMILY: *Picidae*
Features: 4 toes with powerful claws
Location: widely distributed

SUPER FACT:
Woodpeckers can use their beaks for
making music as well as holes.

**The woodpecker's super-strong beak is
totally indestructible!**

Birds of the *Picidae* family—green
woodpeckers, spotted woodpeckers, and the
biggest of all, the black woodpeckers—have an
inbuilt tool: their own hammer drill, in the form of
their beak!

This incredible tool has several uses. When the
male woodpecker wants to seduce a female, it
uses its beak to drum a superfast love song on the
trunk of a tree. Slower knocks to a tree trunk are
used to drill holes for nests or for finding insect
larvae. This useful tool never wears out because
it keeps on growing. To use it, the woodpecker
clings to the trunk in an upright position, gripping
the bark with its powerful claws—two toes at the
front and two at the back—and it also props itself
with its sturdy, muscular tail. To hammer, it vibrates
its neck muscles incredibly fast, and this makes
its head, along with its indestructible beak, move
backward and forward at superfast speed.

SUPERPOWER:
PRECISION DIVING

SUPER STATS:
SCIENTIFIC NAME: *Alcedo atthis*
Habitat: rivers and shallow ponds
Species in decline due to water pollution

SUPER FACT:
This little bird catches fish with almost 100 percent accuracy.

This beautiful blue bird can swoop down on its prey with its eyes closed!

Waiting on its perch above shallow waters, it uses its incredibly sharp eyesight to watch for a fish swimming close to the surface. The second it spots one, it dives superfast, wings tightened against its body to make it completely aerodynamic.

Just before entering the water, the kingfisher closes its eyes! Blue-ish membranes, basically eyelids, close to protect the bird's eyes from the water. The rest of the dive is done blind; the kingfisher relies on the accuracy of its memory of the exact target to skillfully catch its prey. The technique works almost every time!

Having caught its prey, the kingfisher carries the fish back to its perch, knocks it senseless against the branch, and devours it headfirst!

PELICANS

💪 **SUPERPOWER:**
COOPERATIVE FISHING

💡 **SUPER STATS:**
GENUS: *Pelecanus*
Weight: up to 28 pounds (13 kilograms)
Habitat: water
Location: all continents except Antarctica
Almost endangered

👍 **SUPER FACT:**
The great white pelican's beak can be almost 1.6 feet (0.5 meters) long!

Pelicans have developed a clever technique for catching as many fish as they possibly can, and it involves working as a group.

If you watch a group of pelicans for a while, you will see them forming a kind of circle with their huge, open beaks pointing toward the middle. They all then tilt at the same time, plunging their beaks into the water and sticking their tails in the air, like a group of dancers taking a bow! It's very hard indeed for fish to escape this circular trap. The pelican's famous beak has a flexible pouch that acts like a fishing net. Pelicans eat their fish whole, washing them down with powerful digestive juices.

When they want to move to a new spot, they use their large webbed feet to propel them through the water. They also use their feet to glide on the surface when they land.

BANDED ARCHERFISH

SUPERPOWER:
SPITTING INTO THE AIR

SUPER STATS:
SCIENTIFIC NAME: *Toxotes jaculatrix*
Size: up to 12 inches (30 centimeters)
Location: Asia, India, and Australia

SUPER FACT:
This fish can knock down insects with spit!

In the right mouth, spitting can be used as a lethal weapon!

From just under the surface of the water, the banded archerfish looks up to spot an insect on an overhanging leaf. To catch its victim, it uses spit! By positioning its tongue against the roof of its mouth, which has a lengthwise groove along it, the fish can shoot out a jet of water that can travel almost 5 feet (1.5 metres). The fish's aim is to unbalance the insect so that it falls into the water, where the fish can snap it up and swallow it down. As well as a grooved mouth, the banded archerfish has upward-pointing eyes and great 3-D vision, which can adjust between water and air.

The spitting technique is a skill that takes practice. Young banded archerfish have to learn to perfect their aim, and practice to keep getting better.

BEARDED VULTURE

 SUPERPOWER:
IMMACULATE CLEANING

SUPER STATS:
SCIENTIFIC NAME: *Gypaetus barbatus*
Wingspan: nearly 9 feet (2.7 meters)
Weight: 11–15 pounds (5–7 kilograms)
Appearance: orange-breasted;
bearded beak
Location: large mountain ranges

SUPER FACT:
The bearded vulture has the ominous
nickname "bone-breaker!"

This expert eater has powerful digestive juices capable of breaking down bones!

In the mountains, this vulture's exceptional size, orange color, and diamond-shaped tail make it easily recognizable, especially as it tends to live alone. When a sheep or antelope dies somewhere in the mountains, other types of vulture will swoop in first to eat the parts that are easiest to digest. When there's nothing left except the skeleton, only then does the bearded vulture arrive to take charge of the final clean-up. It can swallow most of the bones, which are broken down inside its stomach. If a bone is too big to swallow, the vulture will pick it up and drop it onto a flat rock to break it. Sometimes it loses the bone, but usually it finds all the fragments and greedily swallows them down.

SEA OTTER

 **SUPERPOWER:**
USING CUTLERY

 **SUPER STATS:**
SCIENTIFIC NAME:
Enhydra lutris
FAMILY: *Mustelidae*
Weight: about 66 pounds
(30 kilograms)
Endangered species

 SUPER FACT:
Sea otters are
completely waterproof.

It's not every day you come across an animal that uses tools to eat its food, but the sea otter does!

To find similar behavior in another species, you'd have to look to humans' closest cousins: the great apes.

The sea otter, which lives only on the Pacific coast of North America, goes diving to look for mollusks to eat. It brings a mollusk back up to the surface in a fold of skin—a type of pocket—on its paw. Then, balancing a rock on its chest, it strikes the shell of the mollusk against the rock to break it open.

The sea otter's fur is made up of two layers, making it completely waterproof. The inner layer is fluffy, made of hairs that are constantly oiled by glands in the skin. The hairs of the outer layer are longer and stronger. Lacking a layer of protective fat, these two layers of fur keep it well protected against the cold.

ANGLERFISH

SUPERPOWER:
FATAL ATTRACTION

SUPER STATS:
SCIENTIFIC NAME: *Diceratias pileatus*
Habitat: deep down in the ocean
Size: 8–39 inches (20–100 centimeters)
Weight: about 110 pounds (50 kilograms)

SUPER FACT:
Where these fish live, very deep
underwater, there is no light at all.

**Anglerfish live in total darkness, and catch
their prey by lighting a kind of lamp!**

These deep-sea fish are low-energy fish
that live at depths where prey is scarce.
However, they have perfected a clever
system for catching prey. Hanging
above a female anglerfish's mouth by a
wiry thread is a luminous lantern. Lured
by this strange light, the prey swims close
to her large mouth, and she gobbles it up.
By pulsing the light and waving it about, she
also uses her light to attract a mate.

The sole purpose of the male anglerfish is to
find a female partner for reproduction. Mating
takes place when the male attaches himself
to the female by biting her with his teeth.
Attached to her by the mouth, he then shares
the female's bloodstream!

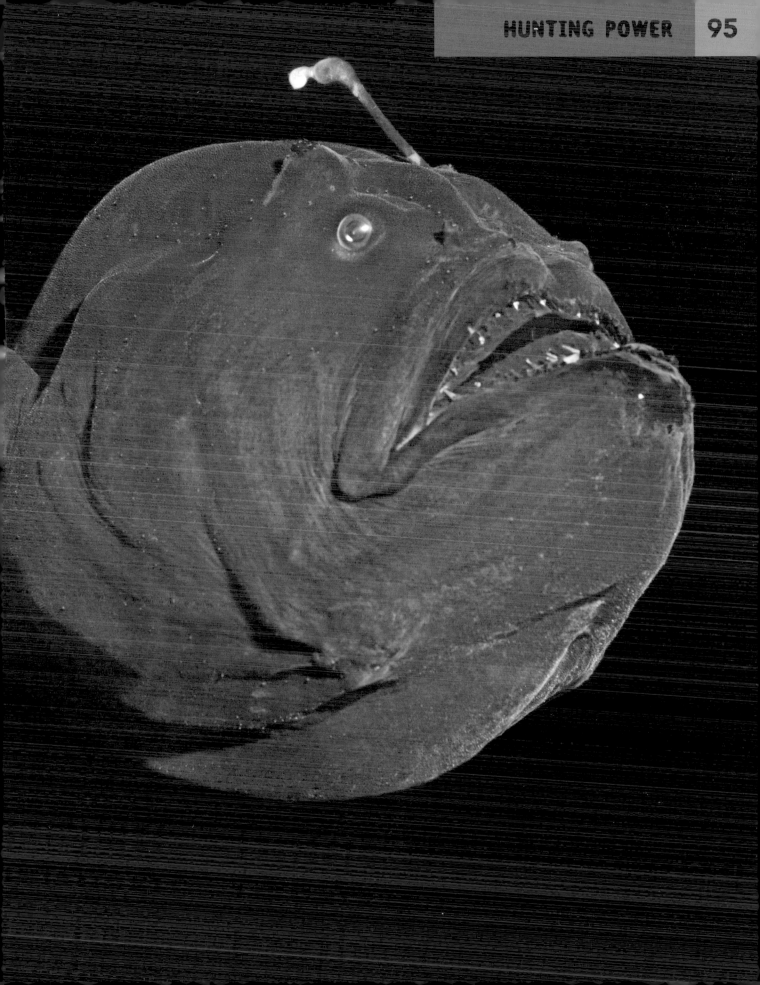

Brimming with creative inspiration, how-to projects, and useful information to enrich your everyday life, quarto.com is a favorite destination for those pursuing their interests and passions.

Inspiring | Educating | Creating | Entertaining

Text © 2022 Quarto Publishing Group USA Inc.
Adapted from original French language text
© 2022 Belles Balades Editions

First published in 2022 by QEB Publishing,
an imprint of The Quarto Group.
100 Cummings Center,
Suite 265D Beverly,
MA 01915, USA.
T (978) 282-9590 F (978) 283-2742
www.quarto.com

Editorial Assistant: Alice Hobbs
Editor: Amber Husain
Design: Starry Dog Books Ltd
Art Director: Susi Martin
Publisher: Holly Willsher

A CIP record for this book is available from the Library of Congress.

ISBN: 978-0-7112-7811-0

9 8 7 6 5 4 3 2 1

Manufactured in Guangdong, China TT062022

PICTURE CREDITS

Adobe Stock/Fotolia: 18/19 Frank Fichtmüller. **Biosphoto:** Back cover: (center) Kim Taylor; 6/7 © Juniors / Biosphoto; 12/13 © Adam Fletcher; 14/15 © Juniors; 20/21 © Nicolas-Alain Petit; 26/27 © Dickie Duckett / FLPA; 32/33 © Mitsuhiko Imamori / Minden Pictures; 34/35 © Thomas Marent / Minden Pictures; 36/37 © Jim Zipp / Ardea; 38/39 © Kim Taylor / Photoshot; 40/41 © J.-M. Labat & F. Rouquette; 42/43 Suzi Eszterhas; 52/53 © Tobias Bernhard Raff; 56/57 © Frederique Olivier / Hedgehog House / Minden Pictures; 58/59 © Matthijs Kuijpers; 62/63 Power and Syred / SPL - Science Photo Library; 66/67 © Christian-Georges Quillivic; 74/75 © Gerhard Koertner / Photoshot; 78/79 © Yva Momatiuk and John Eastcott / Minden Pictures; 84/85 © Michel Poinsignon; 90/91 © John Cancalosi; 92/93 © Norbert Wu / Minden Pictures. **M.Fernandez:** 24/25 © M.Fernandez. **Getty / 13Y5A3:** 70/71 ©AFP-Chris Van Wyk. **Hemis.fr:** 8/9 Valentin Valkov / Alamy; 10/11 Per-Andre HOFFMANN; 16/17 imageBROKER; 30/31 Gerckens-Photo-Hamburg / Shutterstock; 44/45 steve young / Alamy Stock Photo; 46/47 Animals Animals; 64/65 MOIRENC Camille; 76/77 Alamy; 80/81 Minden; 88/89 A & J Visage / Alamy Stock Photo; 94/95 Doug Perrine / Alamy Stock Photo. **Shutterstock:** Front cover: Gerckens-Photo-Hamburg; Back cover: (top) JP74; (bottom left) Ugo Burlini; (bottom right) Dirk Ercken; 1 Coatesy; 2/3 Albert Beukhof; 4/5 duangnapa_b; 22/23 Gerckens-Photo-Hamburg; 28/29 Ciocan Daniel; 48/49 Davydele; 50/51 RealityImages; 54/55 JP74; 60/61 Coatesy; 68/69 Jay Ondreicka; 72/73 ©Alexander Erdbeer; 82/83 Michal Masik; 86/87 Nico Calandra; 96 Naoto Shinkai.